"SEE"
THE EMPOWERING ENERGY SOLUTION

By: Thomas A. Peterson

A SIMPLE & GRAND WAY FOR YOU TO:

Save money today,
Create well paying jobs,
Promote local economic growth,
Reduce energy usage,
Significantly reduce pollution,
Slow any climate change,
Save even more money in the future,
Assure a long-term vibrant economy,
Live & work more comfortably, &
Cut back on foreign energy dependence.

YES, YOU CAN DO ALL OF THIS!

Build New or Convert Existing
Homes & Buildings To Be SEE
(Super Energy Efficient)
Everyone Will Benefit!

A MUST READ FOR EVERY AMERICAN
AS WELL AS EVERYONE ELSE

ISBN-13: 978-1475021400

THIS BOOK IS DEDICATED TO MY YOUNGEST SON,
JORDAN
AND HIS YOUNG CONTEMPORARIES,
WHO WILL REAP THE MOST BENEFITS OF
THE POSITIVE ACTIONS TAKEN
BY THOSE WHO READ THIS BOOK.

MAY WE ALL LOVE AND RESPECT
OUR CHILDREN
AND THEIR FUTURES

THANKS ARE GIVEN TO
EVERYONE
WHO HAD ANYTHING TO DO WITH
TEACHING ME THE SKILLS AND
PROVIDING ME WITH THE KNOWLEDGE
THAT HAS MADE THIS BOOK POSSIBLE.

Table of Contents

INTRODUCTION   6

Chapter 1: WHAT SEE IS ALL ABOUT?   9

Chapter 2: SEE'S MANY BENEFITS   15

Chapter 3: IMMEDIATE SAVINGS CAN PAY FOR SEE!   19

Chapter 4: BENEFIT #1 – SAVINGS ON FUTURE ENERGY

    COSTS   23

Chapter 5: BENEFIT #2 – SIGNIFICANT CUTBACKS ON

    POLLUTION   31

Chapter 6: BENEFIT #3 – SHORT-TERM ECONOMIC

    BENEFITS   35

Chapter 7: BENEFIT #4 – LONG-TERM ECONOMIC

    BENEFITS   37

Chapter 8: BENEFIT #5 – GEO/POLITICAL BENEFITS   39

Chapter 9: BENEFIT #6 – LIVE MORE COMFORTABLY

    IN A SEE HOME   41

Chapter 10: WHO SHOULD SUPPORT SEE?   45

Chapter 11: WHO MIGHT NOT SUPPORT SEE?   49

Chapter 12: WHAT SHOULD YOU DO?   51

Chapter 13: OTHER SEE HOMES THAT I DESIGNED

      AND BUILT   53

AUTHOR'S BIOGRAPHY   61

APPENDICES:

      Appendix A: Energy Savings – New SEE Home

            Vs. New NBC Home   67

      Appendix B: Energy Savings for a New SEE Home

            & ROI   69

      Appendix C: Breakeven Analysis SEE Conversion –

            Financed   71

      Appendix D: ROI for SEE Conversion   73

INTRODUCTION

As a society today, we seem to be confronted with a myriad of problems. Pollution, climate change, rising energy costs, and personal/national/international economic issues (jobs, shrinking value of the dollar/euro, etc.) - - ALL of which our governments and politicians seem incapable of really solving.

The intent of this book is to show that some major solutions really do exist and can empower us as individuals. The ones that I am going to present in this book can actually help with all of the above problems and are relatively simple to achieve. Most importantly, we, as individuals, can take action by ourselves, whether or not politicians or our governments actively support them in any way.

I am going to explain how you, personally, can take actions that will first of all ESSENTIALLY NOT COST YOU ANYTHING, WHILE SAVING YOU MONEY. In the future you will save even more money, as energy costs continue to rise. In addition, they will have a major impact upon cutting back on local and worldwide pollution and averting a possible climate catastrophe. Your actions will also add jobs to your local economy as well as the national economy and help to stabilize those economies both short-term and long-term. These actions should also help to significantly cut-down on any dependence on foreign energy sources. Lastly, they will provide us with more comfortable living and working environments.

Interested? I am now going to briefly explain this simple solution, with the rest of the book providing more details.

The solution is to simply convert our homes and buildings to be Super Energy Efficient - - SEE for short. Such homes will use considerably less energy and, thus, cost less to both heat and cool. New homes can easily be built to SEE standards and, importantly, most of our existing homes can be almost as easily converted or retrofitted to those same SEE standards.

Yes, this will cost money, but it doesn't have to be yours! The energy savings should be greater than the added costs of SEE, and, when financed, the savings will be immediate.

If you are building a new home, the costs for building that home to SEE standards will be about 10% above a traditional new NBC (National Building Code) home. However, if you are financing that new home, the reduced costs of your annual energy expenses will easily pay for the additional finance charges - - every year and more so in the future. The total annual cost of ownership for that new more costly SEE home will simply be less than if it were built as a less costly NBC home.

If you have an older existing home and finance its conversion to SEE standards, energy cost savings will almost always cover the finance charges. The total cost of ownership for that older converted home should again be less than what it was before conversion.

If you want to pay for that SEE conversion of the older home without financing, you may be very surprised with your ROI (Return On Investment). Further, rising energy costs will only make anyone of these scenarios an even better investment over time with ever increasing savings.

Have I got your attention? Then read on! I guarantee that it will be worth your time and, in respect of your time I intentionally have been as simple and brief as I could with this presentation.

Thomas A. Peterson Contact Information

You can find more information about my books here:

Twitter: http://twitter.com/@thomaspeterson9

Facebook: http://www.facebook.com/SEEPublications

Blog: http://seepublications.wordpress.com/

LiberWriter: "SEE" The EMPOWERING Energy Solution

CHAPTER 1: WHAT SEE IS ALL ABOUT?

SEE simply stands for Super Energy Efficient, a term which I coined about five years ago to describe homes and buildings that I, as well as other builders, have been constructing that achieve a high level of energy efficiency. SEE standards are not tied into particular products or specific ways of construction, but are simply a level of energy efficiency that I have proven is easy and economically feasible to achieve. However, the SEE standard is significantly above what the NBC (National Building Code) recommends for new construction standards in the respective states and different regions of the United States. NBC homes and buildings are the type that you have typically observed being built today.

New homes and buildings constructed to SEE standards, by definition, should use one quarter or less of the energy for heating and cooling as do new "well insulated" and conventionally built NBC homes. That represents a seventy-five percent energy saving.

Existing homes built to NBC standards can be retrofitted to the same level of energy efficiency. Older existing homes built with 2x4 construction and various amounts of insulation, when retrofitted to SEE standards, should use one fifth to one tenth of the energy that they used before upgrading.

I developed the SEE standards In the process of building and marketing two medium sized (4 bedroom - 2,100 square foot) homes built on speculation in Southern Maine. I built these two homes using relatively simple energy efficiency building techniques, which I have developed over the past thirty-three years. I became aware of the United States Federal Energy Star Housing Program, which I felt would help me to market these homes. I had them evaluated by an independent home energy evaluator using a HERS (Home Energy Rating System) analysis. This is a necessary step for Energy Star Housing certification. One home was already completed and the other was close to being complete, so I had gotten no advance advice from the energy evaluator, which they readily supply for building such energy efficient homes. Both of these buildings were rated to be "Five Star" Energy Star homes (the highest rating) and were projected to use 74% less energy for heating & cooling than would the same home built to 2005 NBC (National Building Code) insulation standards for Maine.

Actual performance in Southern Maine (7,500 degree-day zone) has verified this lower energy need. Both homes each use about 500 gallons of propane annually for space heating as well as for hot water production. Hot water production for these homes should use about 200 gallons of propane per year, so they were using only about 300 gallons of propane annually for heating. With winter 2011/2012 propane costing about $3.50 per gallon they cost about $1,050.00 to heat or about $3,000.00 less than if they were built as NBC homes. I could easily surpass this performance level today, as I am continually trying to develop better and more economical ways of constructing energy efficient homes and buildings.

Electricity for cooling was not a factor for these homes, as they didn't require any air conditioning as do some new NBC homes built in Maine. In warmer areas of the country where air conditioning is necessary, SEE homes would significantly reduce the amount of electricity used for cooling.

The SEE standard is thus simple:

A SEE HOME NEEDS TO BE HEATED AND/OR COOLED WITH AT LEAST 75% LESS ENERGY THAN AN IDENTICAL CONVENTIONAL "WELL INSULATED" NBC HOME FOR THE STATE OR REGION IN THAT IT IS LOCATED.

I have chosen this 75% number because I have proven that it is an easily achievable standard and, most importantly, cost effective to do so. In other words, SEE will pay for itself with energy savings. I know that it is possible to do better than 75% and encourage any attempts to do so, that is why the SEE standard is stated with "at least 75% less energy".

I also know that there are "zero" energy homes - - especially in Europe. I am also striving to develop such homes myself, but have thus far found that their costs are generally well above what the average homeowner can afford. I couldn't write this book and advocate that such homes paid for the extra financing costs to achieve zero energy use - - at least not at this time. A principle that I heard many years ago still holds true, " It is relatively easy to cut one's energy needs by 75%, but that last 25% will cost you many times what the first 75% cost." That being said, I also do not want to discourage anyone from striving towards developing a zero energy home or building. Whatever is learned through the process will certainly someday be practical to apply to more average SEE homes.

The Energy Star Housing Program goes on to address a home's total energy efficiency going beyond a home's insulation values to also consider a home's appliances, lighting, etc. Another popular program called LEED (Leadership in Energy and Environmental Design) developed by the U.S. Green Building Council goes even farther. With LEED, consideration is given to the overall impact on human and environmental health in the construction of a home or building - - including the building materials used, site development, water savings, indoor environmental quality as well as energy efficiency.

While I also advocate that these additional Energy Star and LEED standards are all also very worthwhile aspects to consider for saving energy in a home or building, I have chosen to keep SEE's emphasis simple. SEE primarily focuses on the insulation values and thermo properties of the building envelop alone - - a comprehensive enough subject in itself.

How to achieve SEE's standards, of course, will vary around the country, state-to-state, and even area-to-area within some particular states. Oregon with 12 gardening zones (formerly six) is one such state. Many different and viable methods are available to achieve SEE's level of performance. The following discussion presents two with which I am personally very familiar.

The two "spec" homes discussed above were built using a modified Canadian "double-wall" system, which was first seen in the 1970's. I have considerably modified the double wall system over the years to improve efficiency as well as to keep construction costs down. I am not promoting any new exotic and unproven technology to achieve SEE standards, although there are certainly some promising newer ones becoming available.

Essentially, those double-wall homes were built with a 2x6 exterior structural wall with R-19 fiberglass insulation. (Note: the higher the R-value of a product, the better the insulating value.) Next I placed a 1" R-5 extruded polystyrene foam board (a.k.a. "blue-board") on all of the exterior walls for a thermo break. I then added a "lightly framed" 2x4 interior wall (studs offset from the exterior wall studs) with additional R-11 fiberglass. I also add a vapor barrier to the middle of this wall system, which serves a dual purpose as it also provides an air infiltration barrier.

While the wall's insulation values add up to R-35, I believe overall wall insulation performance to be closer to R-30, due to thermo breaks because of studs, headers, etc. Similarly, a typical 2x6 R-19/21 fiberglass insulated wall generally has an overall R-value of around R-13. The concrete foundation is insulated with 2" of R-10 extruded polystyrene on the outside and the cap ceiling is insulated with 15" of R-60 blown cellulous. There are certainly some "tricks" as to how I do all of this in a cost and labor efficient manner, but that is beyond the scope of this book. As a general contractor, I have found it relatively easy to instruct or "train" carpenters to build this type of construction. Closer supervision, however, is sometimes required with older carpenters, who I have sometimes found are more "set in their ways".

Another very promising and newer product, with which I have recently become very familiar, is ICF's (Insulated Concrete Forms). To jog people's memory, I jokingly call these "Legos grown up". They are constructed with two layers (inner & outer) of interlocking foam insulation spaced apart with plastic ties (fitting together very much like Legos). Reinforcing steel is placed between the two foam panels followed by poured (often pumped) concrete. This product has been around for at least a few decades now, although it was initially used more for below grade foundation type applications in Maine. Today, they are often used to go up to the roof and at least one manufacturer has a similar system that can even be used for roofs. The typical wall product promoted by most manufacturers has an overall insulating value of R-22.

However, I am very familiar with a manufacturer that has a great product with an insulating value of R-30, that would more easily come up to SEE standards - - at least for Maine. This same manufacturer also has even higher R-value wall system products.

Experienced carpenters can easily learn how to build ICF homes, but there may be some reluctance as working with steel and concrete is quite different from working exclusively with typical wood construction. However, there are plenty of builders who are familiar with ICF construction in Maine and I am sure around the rest of the country as well.

There are certainly many variations in the two methods that I have briefly discussed above for building new homes. The purpose of this book, however, is not to provide a detailed construction manual. I just want to explain that proven great products already exist and that there are builders who routinely use them for SEE-type construction.

Older existing homes each offer more unique individual challenges. These challenges, however, can be met whether one chooses a more expensive "gut rehab" or a simpler and generally less costly upgrade of the insulation and doors & windows on the exterior walls of the home. Such upgrades can be generally done with wood construction; however, one ICF manufacturer of which I am very familiar has a great exterior interlocking foam product. There are also other very promising products that can achieve SEE standards, but again, providing a detailed comprehensive construction manual is not the purpose of this book.

My purpose in this chapter is to simply explain the SEE standard and show that such construction, with readily available and existing products, is easily applicable to new as well as existing homes and buildings. I also want to emphasize that SEE construction will save significantly on energy usage and cost, as will be well explained in more detail in later chapters.

Double-Wall SEE Homes Described Above

Windham, Maine (Author in foreground)

Chapter 2: SEE'S MANY BENEFITS

The benefits of SEE are many and astoundingly broad in scope.

The last chapter should make one of SEE's major benefits very clear - - saving money. The owner of a SEE home or building will use considerably less energy than one not originally built or upgraded to SEE standards. Thus, it will cost significantly less to pay for the energy that is required to heat and cool a SEE home. As I am writing this book in early 2012, fuel oil and propane prices are running in the mid three-dollar range in Maine and appear like they may well go much higher. Thus, the savings for heating can easily run into the thousands of dollars annually in a moderate to colder climate. In warmer climates, similar savings can often be realized through the use of less electricity for air conditioning. These savings will benefit all of us in many diverse ways.

The first benefit of SEE is that the energy cost savings can immediately pay for SEE. If a new SEE home or building is conventionally financed, savings should easily cover the additional financing costs for the10% more expensive SEE structure - - in the first year of occupancy. In other words, the total cost of ownership for a more expensive SEE home is less than for an identical less expensive NBC home.   If not financed, the ROI (return on investment) on the 10% extra cost for a SEE building is somewhere around 15%.   Converting older existing buildings to SEE standards is also generally financially feasible and the ROI can be equally enticing. In a later chapter, I will discuss this area in much more detail.

A second benefit of SEE is that the savings that SEE achieves will actually get much larger over time. This is simply the result of rising energy costs. Thus, SEE homes and buildings offer their owners a significant hedge against rising energy costs. Again, this is discussed in much more detail in a later chapter.

A third benefit of SEE is, that by using considerably less energy, SEE homes will cause considerably less pollution of our environment. Each SEE home will annually cutback on the greenhouse gasses CO_2 and NO_x, as well as other health threatening pollution products. Again, a later chapter will provide more detail on this subject.

A fourth benefit of SEE is the immediate or short-term local and national economic benefits of beginning to convert our homes and buildings to SEE standards. This process will create many well-paying jobs - - in construction, product manufacturing, materials supply, as well as in transportation. A new SEE home, apartment, or building will require around 10% more materials and labor to produce than conventional new NBC structures. However, we are currently in a new housing slump. What is much more important right now is that the conversion of our older existing buildings to SEE standards could create immediate jobs and literally begin a whole new industry in the United States - - SEE retrofits / conversions. Most of the well-paying jobs created will be "un-exportable" construction jobs that will be evenly dispersed throughout the United States wherever there are homes or buildings. These new jobs will last for decades, of course, as it will take some time to convert all of our existing homes and buildings to SEE standards.

A fifth benefit of SEE is the long-term economic benefit that will be bestowed upon all segments of our society. If energy costs continue to be high or most likely increase, they will drain the economic vitality from our society. If I own a SEE home that costs me $1,000.00 a year to heat & cool and my neighbor owns an identical "well insulated" NBC home that costs $4,000.00 to heat and cool, I can assure you that I will be eating out more frequently and buying more products & services that our society offers than will my neighbor.

If energy costs double, I will have to spend $2,000.00 on energy, while my neighbor will be spending $8,000.00. Energy companies will simply be taking in the dollars, that would most likely be otherwise spent in our local economies - - draining their vitality. If we don't convert our homes and buildings to SEE, all of our economic futures will be much bleaker.

A sixth benefit of SEE homes & buildings is that in needing less energy; we will be less dependent upon more distant foreign energy sources. I will let others with more expertise in this geo/political area than me promote the benefits of this. However, keeping things closer to home always looks like a benefit to me for many reasons.

A seventh benefit of SEE is that homes and buildings built to SEE standards are much more comfortable in which to live or work. Room temperatures are more even, they are quieter buildings insulated from outside noises, and there are less internal mechanical noises.

SEE is simply a win/win/win/win/win/win/win (or win to the 7th power) situation for all of us. Even the oil companies, that may fear reduced fuel sales with SEE homes & buildings, will be able to convert their raw materials into energy saving foam insulation to support the transformation to SEE homes and buildings. Also, people with more and better jobs will be spending more money on fuel for travel, for work (to and from construction jobs alone), as well as for leisure.

A couple of years ago I met two very environmentally conscious high school seniors from Yarmouth, Maine, who were receiving public recognition awards for their environmental actions. In a brief meeting with them, I explained the SEE program to them. Their response was quite simple, "It's a No-Brainer!" With everything that I have said about SEE thus far, I am sure that you will agree. Lets now look at the benefits of SEE in more detail.

Chapter 3: Benefit #1 - IMMEDIATE SAVINGS CAN PAY FOR SEE!

"ADAPTING SEE STANDARDS FOR OUR NEW AND EXISTING HOMES AND BUILDINGS DOES NOT HAVE TO COST US ANYTHING!" Thomas A. Peterson 1/1/12

Many people to whom I have presented the arguments in the preceding chapters for SEE, often come back with a response similar to, "But I can't afford the 10% more for a new home, or such a major expense to convert my existing home or building to SEE standards!" My simple response is, "You REALLY can't afford not to build your new home or convert your existing home or buildings to SEE standards."

The reasons for this are quite simple. The cost of the energy saved should cover the cost of financing the building of new or converting of existing homes AND buildings to SEE standards. If not financed, the ROI (Return on Investment) of the cost of meeting SEE standards for a new or existing structure is generally quite acceptable, if not outstanding, compared to most of today's other investment opportunities.

For new construction, energy savings should easily cover the extra 10% cost, required to build and/or finance a new SEE structure. This means that at the end of the first year you occupy your new SEE home or building, you will have more money in your bank account than if it were not built as a SEE structure. In other words, the "cost of ownership" for the "10% more expensive" SEE building is less than for a similar "10% less expensive" NBC building. The lower cost of ownership will continue and also be even greater in the future. The next chapter explains this in much more detail.

Most mortgage companies also recognize what I have said above and thus have special lending programs for energy efficient homes. These programs often allow a higher debt to income ratio, as mortgage companies understand that the owners of energy efficient homes have a lower cost of ownership and thus will be spending much less on energy to live in their homes.

Another way to look at a SEE home's performance is to compare it to a relatively new, but highly accepted energy efficient product in our culture today - - an energy efficient hybrid car. In 2012, Toyota makes a Camry LE that gets 28 mpg (combined city/highway) and a Camry LE Hybrid that gets 41 mpg (combined city/highway). The hybrid car costs 10% more, but uses 32% less fuel than the non-hybrid car per mile travelled. Similarly, a SEE home costs 10% more than an NBC home, but uses 75% less energy for heating and cooling. If a hybrid car is an accepted way to save on energy use in our society, shouldn't a SEE home be more acceptable? People in our society simply don't know the facts, which is why this book is being written.

For an existing home or building, your energy cost savings will most likely cover any financing costs to convert it or retrofit it up to SEE standards. In both cases, a HERS analysis - - done before any decisions are made or construction begins - - should answer any skeptic's concerns.

Let's look at this all in a bit more depth.

NEW CONSTRUCTION:

Let's say building a new structure to SEE standards will add 10% or $20,000.00 to the cost of a $200,000.00 home or building. Lets further say that a HERS analysis for that building shows that the structure, if built as an NBC building, will use $4,000.00 of energy annually for heating & cooling. The same structure built to SEE standards, by definition, would use 1/4 as much energy ($1,000.00) and thus save $3,000.00. If the project were to be financed over 30 years at a rate of 5%, the added annual costs of financing $20,000.00 would be $1,288.32. The $3,000.00 savings minus the added financing costs of $1,288.32 yields a net savings of $1,711.68 - - in the first year of ownership!

Chapter 4 goes into more detail of what savings could result in later years as energy costs inevitably rise.

A businessperson might look at these savings in a slightly different manner - - from an ROI (Return on Investment) perspective. It might benefit some homeowners to also consider SEE from an ROI standpoint. If one were to consider the extra $20,000.00 cost of meeting SEE standards as an investment, the $3,000.00 annual savings would be the return on that investment. ROI is generally shown as a percentage, thus the $3,000.00 savings divided by the $20,000.00 investment would yield an ROI of 15%. This should beat your savings account interest rate of something probably less than 1%, if not the rates of most of today's other investments (CD's, bonds, stock market, etc.). Should energy costs ever double, so would your ROI - - going to 30%. Also realize that there will be no capital gains or other taxes on that ROI. Again, Chapter 4 may astound you with what the ROI may rise to in future years.

OLDER / EXISTING CONSTRUCTION:

With an existing home or building, the cost of doing a SEE conversion/retrofit is slightly more complicated than for new construction. This is simply because each older structure will present its own unique construction issues with which to address to bring the home or building up to SEE standards. Thus, the costs of a SEE conversion may vary much more than for a new structure. However, the costs of the unique proposed SEE improvements can be estimated and then used to help determine if a SEE conversion would be worth doing.

Next, a HERS analysis can be done for the existing structure. Further, the actual past history of its energy use/costs can be determined. A second HERS analysis evaluating the effects of the proposed SEE retrofit changes to that building will tell you what energy savings will result from such a conversion. As for new construction, if the potential energy savings cover or more than cover the cost of financing the SEE retrofit, the conversion is worth doing.

In some cases, while a SEE conversion might not appear worthwhile today, the future may well make it much more appealing. This is because the potential savings will rise along with rises in energy prices. I believe that every structurally sound building will eventually be worth having a SEE retrofit - - maybe sooner than you might think. Chapter 4 again provides more in-depth reasons for this.

As for new construction, one can also take an ROI perspective on a SEE conversion. One need only take the projected energy savings and divide them by the cost of the SEE conversion. If the proposed SEE improvements for a particular building do not provide an acceptable ROI, one simply does not undertake the improvements. In most cases an acceptable ROI will be presented. If not, rising energy costs again may make the ROI more acceptable in the future. For example, if a $50,000.00 conversion to SEE were to save $3,000.00 on energy costs today, it would provide a 6% ROI. While 6% might not be an enticing ROI to some, the doubling of energy costs would bring the ROI up to what might be a much more enticing 12%. Again, at some point in the future, rising energy costs will make a SEE conversion very enticing for every home and building owner, if not mandatory to continue to afford to use the structure.

Honestly, with some older existing homes or buildings, it may not be worth the expense of converting to SEE. This is because an existing structure may be too old, decrepit or poorly built and, thus, not worth the investment in converting it to SEE standards. Doing expensive bodywork for a "rolled over" five-year old car makes sense, while doing it for a twenty-year old "Junker" probably would not.

SUMMARY:

To summarize this chapter, the energy savings of building new or converting older homes and buildings to SEE standards should cover any additional financing costs to achieve such standards. Again this can be determined before construction begins with a HERS analysis. If you want to consider an ROI approach, the rate of return you get on the SEE "investment" should be very enticing compared to what most other investments offer today. Tomorrow's energy savings should look even better, again, as the next chapter will show in detail.

Chapter 4: Benefit #2 – SAVINGS ON FUTURE ENERGY COSTS

Saving on energy usage and its corresponding costs should provide an immediate benefit to the owner of a SEE property, as discussed in the last chapter. The longer-term savings should be ever increasing and much greater. This is simply because rising energy prices will continually multiply those savings.

To begin such an analysis, one needs to have some idea of future energy costs. For this, I researched petroleum energy product costs over the past 35 years. Natural gas and electricity certainly have had similar if slightly lower rates of increase. From 1976 to 2007 (30 years), petroleum based energy costs rose 500% (obviously with some spikes and dips along the way). This 500% increase averaged about 5.5 % per year, or about the rate of inflation over that time period.

However, annual rates of increase accelerated near the end of that period. From 1999 to 2007, the annual rise in fuel oil costs averaged 12.0 % per year. Between January of 2007 and January of 2012 fuel oil prices again averaged a 12.0 % annual increase (again with spikes and dips). Since there has been an average increase of 12.0 % per year since 1999, I feel that this is an appropriate rate to use for analyzing the future. Many energy analysts believe a much higher rate of price increases may occur, as demand increases while supplies dwindle.

For a mortgage interest rate, I used 5.0 %. Currently, secondary market rates are around 3.75% and local bank "in-house" portfolio rates are around 6% (going rates on 1/1/12). These rates are for fixed rate mortgages. I believe 5.0 % to be arbitrary, but a good "middle ground" for the purposes of this analysis.

There are four tables (A, B, C, & D) presented in the Appendix that support the following discussions. I have tried to make this analysis as simple as possible, but if necessary, you could talk to a banker or a financial advisor to help you understand these tables and what I am going to point out about them.

To begin this discussion from a more simple perspective, I will start by showing the energy cost savings for a new SEE home or building versus a new NBC structure. Following that, I will look at what older existing homes and buildings can offer for energy cost savings when converted to SEE standards. To provide some deeper insight for both new and existing construction, I have also provided a complementary ROI or "investment" analysis for both.

NEW CONSTRUCTION – Financed:

The following analysis is based on the figures presented on the table in Appendix A.

As stated earlier, a new SEE home should cost around 10% more than an NBC home. This means that a $200,000.00 NBC home would cost about $220,00.00, if built as a SEE home - - $20,000.00 or 10% more. With a standard 30-year fixed rate mortgage (typical for a new home) at 5.0 %, the additional costs for financing that $20,000.00 would be $107.36 per month or $1,288.32 per year. The projected energy savings for that home in the first year are $3,000.00. That amount would cover the extra interest payments of $1,288.32 and leave you with a net savings of $1,711.68 to spend or keep in your bank account.

This analysis does not consider any tax benefits for paying the additional interest on the $20,000.00. It also does not account for any increased homeowner equity from paying down the principle on the extra $20,000.00 financed.

24

The longer-term savings grow and the annual amount saved minus the additional mortgage payments becomes quite astounding. See the Annual Net Savings For SEE Home column in Appendix A. This happens because of two reasons; 1) energy costs will probably rise at around 12.0 % annually, but 2) your fixed rate mortgage payment will stay the same.

In year 10, your energy costs for your SEE home/building will probably have risen to $2,773.08. Your NBC neighbor's energy costs will be $11,092.32, which means that you will have spent $8,319.24 less than your neighbor for energy that year. Subtracting your fixed extra annual financial costs of $1,288.32, results in your having saved $7,030.92 that year over what your NBC neighbor had to pay to live in an identical home.

Using the same analysis, in year 20 your net savings over your NBC neighbor will have risen to $24,549.97 - - assuming that your neighbor hasn't yet converted his home to SEE standards. Year 30 net savings are $78,961.47. However, your neighbor probably either went bankrupt or someone else bought his home and brought it up to SEE standards.

Additional things to note from Appendix A are that:

1. By year 16, the energy savings of $15,132.38 cover the total annual cost of the mortgage on the home of $14,172.12.

2. By year 30, the cumulative energy savings (or total energy savings) of $685,348.45 are 161% of the total mortgage payments of $425,163.60 over 30 years.

3. You will have given the energy companies $723,998.05 less ($965,330.74 minus $241,332.68) than your NBC neighbor over the 30 years of your mortgage.

4. You will have saved $685,348.45, while having paid only $38,649.60 extra in mortgage payments over the 30 years of your mortgage.

To summarize; the annual cost of ownership for a financed SEE home or building is initially less than for an NBC building and it only gets better, much better over time.

NEW CONSTRUCTION – INVESTED (Not Financed):

Building to SEE standards can also be looked at from an ROI viewpoint. Most business people would look at it from this perspective, but a prospective homeowner building a new home may also want to look at it this way. This would be especially true for someone that might not need or want a traditional mortgage (for example: someone downsizing and/or retiring).

The table in Appendix B supports this discussion. Again for simplicity, this table assumes the same SEE and NBC homes as used in Appendix A. Thus, note that the energy savings of a SEE home over an NBC home are identical to those shown in Appendix A. To calculate the ROI, the annual energy savings are simply divided by the extra $20,000.00 cost of building a SEE over an NBC home. As stated earlier, in year 1 the ROI would be 15.0% ($3,000.00/$20,000.00). As energy costs rise in subsequent years, the dollar savings amount grows and correspondingly the ROI grows as a percentage of the invested $20,000.00. By year 5 your annual ROI has increased to 23.6 %, by year 10 to 41.6 %, by year 15 to 73.3 %, by year 20, to 129.2 %, etc. Over the 30-year life of the mortgage the $20,000.00 SEE "investment" will have saved you $776,664.26 - - over 3/4 of a million dollars!

What other investments do you know of that can provide those rates of return? Should you leave your savings in 1) a 2% CD, 2) the low yielding bond market, 3) the risky stock market, or 4) an investment that provides a 15.0 % ROI in its first year with the ROI only increasing in subsequent years. Also note that the SEE "investment" is continually working as a hedge against any future rise in energy costs?

Again note that there are no capital gains taxes on those increasing savings. Your SEE ROI is essentially tax-free! Remember the "No Brainer" comment of the high school students mentioned earlier.

OLDER EXISTING CONSTRUCTION – Financed:

Converting an older existing home to SEE standards needs to be looked at somewhat differently than for new construction. Generally, one can utilize a breakeven analysis to determine whether a proposed SEE conversion is worth doing, which it generally is.

The breakeven point is the amount of money that can be financed where the energy savings will cover the financing costs. In other words, "X" amount of annual energy savings would cover the annual financial costs of a "Y" amount loan for "Z" number of years.

One begins by estimating what needs to be done for a SEE conversion and what it will cost. Then the energy efficiency (inefficiency) of the existing structure is evaluated along with gathering actual past energy use data. This is followed by a HERS analysis that will determine what energy savings will result from the proposed SEE conversion. This HERS analysis might also be used to "fine tune" what needs to be done for the SEE conversion. The end result of this analysis is the amount of energy usage and costs that the proposed SEE conversion will save.

Then the breakeven analysis is done, which will determine the maximum amount that can be financed at current interest rates with the anticipated savings.

For example: lets take an older 2x4 home that is almost identical in size/shape to the new homes used in the above example. This older home will probably have at most R-11 insulation and use about 50% more energy than a new 2x6 NBC home. Thus, this older home probably uses about $6,000.00 annually to heat & cool. Bringing it up to SEE standards should bring those costs down to $1,000.00 - - resulting in an annual savings of $5,000.00. The HERS analysis would be used to confirm this.

The table in Appendix C provides a breakeven analysis for the above example. For comparison purposes it shows a breakeven comparison between a 15-year and a 30-year note. Such a SEE conversion loan could be taken out for several different periods (typically 5, 10, 15, 20, 25 & 30 years) depending upon the financial capabilities, and needs or desires of the borrower. Since a SEE conversion would be a major investment, 15 years would be reasonable and 30 years could be used if necessary to make the financing work. Such a loan could also be tied into a total refinancing of the home at a lower interest rate, if it were in the borrower's best interest.

If one were to get a 15-year secondary market mortgage at 3.75 % (going rate on 1/1/12), the $5,000.00 energy savings would cover $57,300.00 worth of SEE improvements. A 30-year 3.75 % mortgage would cover $90,000.00 worth of SEE improvements.

A 15-year in-house (portfolio) mortgage @ 6.0 % (going rate on 1/1/12) would cover $49,400.00 worth of SEE improvements. A 30-year 6.0 % mortgage would cover $69,500.00 worth of SEE improvements.

For comparison and simplicity purposes, the table in Appendix C uses a 5.0 % interest rate and periods of 15 and 30 years. Again, the exact scenario one would consider would depend upon an individual borrower's situation and personal choice, as well as the structure being converted to SEE standards and the financing rates at the time of the conversion.

The breakeven points in Appendix C would be the $52,700.00 for 15 years and $77,600.00 for 30 years at today's energy prices. This breakeven analysis shows the amount one could spend/invest and, as long as the financial costs of the SEE improvements cost that amount or less, one would breakeven or save money doing the SEE conversion.

Rising energy costs (as presented in Appendix C) will continually raise the breakeven point. If energy costs, as projected, double in seven years, the above breakeven costs of improvements would be $104,000.00 for 15 years and $153,000.00 for 30 years, respectively. Rising energy costs will eventually make a SEE conversion financially practical, if not necessary, for almost every existing home and building. Once an existing home is converted to SEE, as for a new SEE home, the future energy savings will continue to rise and probably astound you.

If one were to be purchasing an existing home, one could also consider wrapping SEE conversion costs into the original mortgage. Depending on the condition of the home that they were buying, they might end up with a SEE home with possibly a totally new exterior. All these improvements and benefits with the annual cost of ownership less than if they didn't do the SEE conversion.

Another thing to consider with an older building is that, if there is a need for that building to be resided, reroofed, or to have older windows and doors replaced, the costs of achieving SEE standards would be reduced by those already needed and/or possibly planned costs.

If any major exterior renovation work is being planned on a home or building, one should definitely consider having a SEE conversion done at the same time.

OLDER EXISTING CONSTRUCTION – Invested (Not Financed):

Again, an ROI analysis may help to evaluate the value of converting an existing home or building to SEE standards. The table in Appendix D will help to explain this method of evaluation for an existing structure. For simple comparison purposes, I have chosen two costs for the SEE renovation - - $50,000.00 and $75,000.00.

Assuming the same home as used for Appendix C with the same $5,000.00 energy savings projected for year-1, the ROI for a $50,000.00 conversion would be 10.0 %. A more expensive conversion of $75,000.00 would still provide an ROI of 6.67 % - - again for year-1. Rising energy costs will mean a rising ROI, the same as for new construction. For year-5, the ROI for the $50,000.00 conversion should have risen to 15.74 %, and the $75,000.00 ROI would have risen to 10.49 %. Note how rapidly the respective ROI's rise after year-5.

If, as a homeowner, you had a $50,000.00 or $75,000.00 CD, savings account, or other investment, would you be getting a better interest rate or ROI on them? Would that ROI also be non-taxable, as would the savings from a SEE conversion? Would it also provide you with a hedge against future energy cost inflation?

Apartment owners in particular should consider SEE for converting their older existing buildings and especially for any new construction. This would be even more of a consideration, if they provide free heat or cooling for their rental units. With rising energy costs, they could afford to keep their rents lower than their rental competition, thus assuring higher occupancy rates. Or, rising rental rates in their market would simply mean a higher profit margin on their rentals.

CHAPTER SUMMARY:

In the four evaluations of SEE used above, I believe that I have made a pretty compelling argument as to why every home and building owner should at the least consider living in or owning a SEE building.

Your individual financial position will determine if a new SEE home or building, or conversion of an existing one is the right thing for you to do. At least now you know the potential savings that SEE could provide. You should also know your future energy costs should you decide to put off converting to SEE and can budget accordingly for higher and higher energy bills. SEE homes and buildings simply offer a significant hedge against energy cost inflation. Remember the "No brainer" comment of the high school students.

Past performance is no guarantee of future performance, but I do not foresee lower energy costs in our future.

Chapter 5: Benefit #3 – SIGNIFICANT CUTBACKS ON POLLUTION

SEE homes produce significantly less pollution than do newer NBC or older non-SEE homes and buildings. It's a simple relationship; the less energy you use, the less pollution you create. But, as with your monetary savings, how much less pollution you create with a SEE home may astound you.

The two SEE homes first presented in Chapter 1 and discussed throughout this book were analyzed with a HERS analysis as part of their Energy Star approval process. As "Five Star" Energy Star homes, each home was individually projected to produce 10,632 pounds less of carbon dioxide (CO_2) annually, as well as 13.5 pounds less of nitrogen oxides (NO_x), and 3.9 pounds less of sulfur dioxide (SO_2), than would an identical NBC home.

Both carbon dioxide and nitrogen oxides are known greenhouse gases. While the reduction in the amount of nitrogen oxides produced are much smaller than for carbon dioxide, nitrogen oxides produce 298 times the greenhouse effect (over a 100 year period) than does carbon dioxide. In addition, nitrogen oxides stay in the atmosphere much longer than does carbon dioxide. The annual 13.5 pounds of nitrous oxide have the equivalent greenhouse effect of 4,023 pounds of carbon dioxide.

Sulfur dioxide is a highly reactive gas that is known for its adverse health effects upon humans - - especially on the respiratory system.

Acid rain is produced by both nitrous oxides and sulfur dioxide.

Remember, that these pollution cutbacks are annual and will continue every tear for the life of the SEE home or building - - perhaps for 100 years or more. Just think a single SEE home's ability to save 10,000 pounds of carbon dioxide pollution annually over 100 years totals one million pounds.

Most people are not aware of the fact that 40% of the energy used in the United States is used to heat and cool our homes and places of business. If these buildings were to be all converted to SEE standards, the reduction in energy used in the U.S. would probably be decreased by at least 20%, if not 30%. There would also be a corresponding reduction in pollution by that amount.

Conversion to SEE cannot be done "overnight"; however, a concerted effort could probably achieve that energy/pollution savings over twenty years (give or take a few). Remember it will have to be done one home or building at a time. Want to help and be one of the leaders in this pollution reduction effort? Oh, and don't forget all of the money you will also save!

Oil lobbyists keep pushing for the opening up of the North Slope of Alaska. Such an action has been estimated to be able to supply 2% of the United State's total energy needs, but only until this resource is expected to run out in 20 years or so.

While converting all of our homes and buildings to SEE may take 20 years, we are talking about a 20-30% cutback in United States energy use, which will last the lifetime of the SEE home or building - - probably at least 100 years, if not longer. Where are the lobbyists for SEE? We ALL need to get going on this!

I must also comment on the stories being touted on how the Earth's warming could be part of a "natural cycle" and not due to human activity. It may or may not be. However, that statement seems to somehow imply to me, at least, that we should not feel compelled to worry or do anything about this. I cannot agree less with this.

32

There are two simple facts that I would like to have you consider regarding this. The first is that since the Industrial Revolution began the amount of carbon dioxide in our atmosphere has increased by almost 40% going from 280 ppm (parts per million) to 390 ppm - - figured to be due primarily to the burning of fossil fuels. The second fact is that atmospheric scientists have proven through studying the Earth's ancient history (Antarctic & Greenland ice cores, etc.) that carbon dioxide does help to hold the Earth's warmth from radiating back out into space. Given these two facts, the carbon dioxide that humans have and are continuing to add to the atmosphere of the Earth surely will, over time, be making the planet warmer than it would otherwise be. You don't have to be a scientist to determine this; it just takes common sense.

Now, suppose that the Earth's warming is part of a natural cycle, just like an asteroid or comet hitting the Earth would be part of a natural Earth/solar system cycle. A simple look at our moon will confirm this. In the case of an asteroid or comet, would we not, as a human race, do all that we have the capability of doing to avert that catastrophe? The Earth's warming will also have catastrophic effects from rising ocean levels to possible major climate shifts. Should we not, as a human race, likewise do all that we have the capability of doing to alter that catastrophe?

If we continue to trash the Earth, where will we go? The Earth will survive whatever we choose to do to it, but life, as we now know it, including the human race, may not. The destruction of the polar bears' environment is only the beginning, The Earth as it is now can support up to eight billion people. We are currently at about seven billion. If sea levels rise 50 feet, as predicted by some climatological models, the Earth's capacity to agriculturally support humans will be reduced to as little as two billion - - at least according to a recent History Channel program. What will happen to the other five to six billion people? I am not sure that a moon colony, as proposed by a 2012 presidential candidate, could ever support that many people.

Yes, I will be concerned about our environment as long as I am here. Where else can our children or I practically go?

Chapter 6: Benefit #4 – SHORT-TERM ECONOMIC BENEFITS

We are currently in a severe economic recession in the United States and worldwide. Converting or retrofitting our existing homes and buildings to SEE standards could easily help to bring us out of that economic situation - - almost immediately. Constructing new SEE homes and buildings will naturally follow in time. History shows that no U.S. recession has ever ended without construction and housing leading the way.

The current economic situation has created a major slump in the total U.S. construction industry, which has certainly had a major negative affect upon many aspects of our economy. Obviously, construction companies and their workers and subcontractors have all been negatively affected, but so have materials manufacturers, materials suppliers (wholesale & retail), and the transportation industry. If we began a major program to retrofit our homes and buildings to SEE standards, well paying jobs in all of these sectors of the economy would quickly be created. Tens, if not hundreds of thousands of jobs could be created almost immediately with many more to follow. These well paying jobs would also greatly help to rebuild our shrunken middle-class.

These jobs would be created evenly throughout the United States - - wherever there are already existing homes and buildings. They would also be "un-exportable" jobs without, for the most part, *Made in China* stamped on them (nails & screws sometimes being the exception).

What I am proposing here is the development of a whole new industry in the United States and beyond - - **converting our existing homes & buildings to SEE standards.** Obviously, this will not be a small or quick task, but it eventually will be a necessary task for economic, if not environmental reasons.

The scenario for an economic recovery with SEE is actually quite simple. A smart home or building owner decides to have their building converted to SEE standards. A local builder will be chosen to do the work and jobs for unemployed and underemployed carpenters and other construction workers will be created. Materials will be purchased from local building supply companies, who will also need to hire sales personnel, truck drivers and yard workers creating more jobs. Materials manufacturers will have to increase their production of products and more jobs will be created - - probably somewhat less locally. The transportation industry will have more deliveries to make from manufacturers to building supply companies and again more jobs will be created.

The workers in these new jobs will now have money to spend in restaurants, at convenience stores, gas stations, retail outlets, auto dealers, etcetera; creating still more jobs. And don't forget the person who had their home converted to SEE, he/she will also have more money to spend locally. With all of these new workers, government tax revenues (income, sales, business, etc.) will rise, so better services will be able to be provided - - perhaps creating even more jobs. As more people convert their homes and buildings to SEE, more people will become aware of the benefits of SEE and more will want their buildings converted. **EVERYONE WILL SIMPLY WIN**, we just need to begin the process of converting to SEE. And just think energy savings will actually pay for this all to happen!

How can our politicians and our governments not support the establishment of such an economic solution as SEE provides. Shouldn't they be voraciously promoting it? If they don't, we can simply do it for our own personal economic gain, a hedge against future energy cost inflation, or just to feel that we are doing something good for our neighbors, the local & national economy and our environment.

Or, we can simply do it for all of these reasons at the same time.

Chapter 7: Benefit #5 – LONG-TERM ECONOMIC BENEFITS

The long-term economic future that SEE offers us is also very bright. As the last chapter explained, as we convert more and more of our homes and buildings to SEE standards, those doing so will have more money to either 1) save and invest, or 2) to spend on the other goods and services that our local, national, and global economies provide. This will continue year after year. The extra money, that the growing number of SEE home and building owners will have, will continually become ever greater over that of their neighboring NBC and older non-SEE building owners.

The new SEE conversion industry will continue to expand and grow, along with new homes and buildings being constructed more and more to SEE standards. The many new and well paying jobs being created will continue to increase especially through the new SEE conversion industry. Any unemployed, underemployed, and new workers will continue to find better paying jobs pumping more money into our economy. These jobs will be mostly local and for the most part "non-exportable"; as opposed to the many other U.S. manufacturing jobs that we have seen go overseas.

The driving force behind this new economy will not end in the foreseeable future and the benefits will continue to multiply for people as well as for businesses. All of these factors will contribute to the rebuilding of our middle class, a larger tax base for our governments, and a long-term bright economic future for all of us.

My intent is to be positive with what I am presenting in this book, but perhaps a look at what will happen if we do not follow the economic path that SEE offers is worth considering. Briefly, not converting to SEE will provide a much bleaker economic picture. Unfortunately, I see no alternative other than a continued long-term downward spiraling economic slump, as rising energy costs (maybe sporadically, but surely continually) drain our personal finances and our economy of its potential vitality.

How can anyone not support or vote to follow the path that SEE offers?

Chapter 8: Benefit #6 – GEO/POLITICAL BENEFITS

Building new and converting our older existing homes and buildings to SEE standards will mean that we will gradually be using less and less energy for heating and cooling our homes in the United States than we would otherwise. This should result in less dependence on foreign energy sources and, thus, we will be able to rely more and more on our local energy resources. The United States will also become much less of a source of global pollution - - especially greenhouse gases and acid rain. To fully and adequately explain the multiple benefits from a geo/political standpoint is way beyond the realm of this book and, truthfully, my expertise.

However, as a longtime observer of world politics, I have to believe that there are a myriad of ways that the United States or any other nation having less dependence on foreign energy sources, will be a benefit. Reducing global pollution will also help to lessen the need for much of the geo/political intrigue that we see in our world today.

Perhaps T. Boone Pickens could help to enlighten us more here. As the developer of the Pickens' Plan, which strongly advocates reducing United States' dependence on foreign energy sources, I am sure that Mr. Pickens has well thought out and documented the many negative aspects that relying on foreign energy sources imposes on the United States or for that matter any other nation.

Chapter 9: Benefit #7 – LIVE MORE COMFORTABLY IN A SEE HOME

One will find that living in a SEE home or working in a SEE building is physically a much more pleasant and comfortable experience than what an NBC building would provide. The benefits of that extra insulation go well beyond just the energy and monetary savings.

A SEE building is simply more evenly cooler in the summer and more evenly warmer in the winter than are NBC structures. See buildings are also much less "drafty" than NBC buildings. This is not just due to the fact that they are more tightly built, but because they also have much less differences in temperatures between the floor and ceiling, which can cause internal air movement (a.k.a. drafts). The reason for less drafts is due to the natural heating and cooling dynamics of a SEE building being much different than that of an NBC building with which most of us are much more familiar.

In an NBC building a much greater volume of cooler air is cascading down the exterior walls during colder seasons, than in a SEE building. During warmer seasons the NBC building has a greater volume of warmer air rising up those same exterior walls. The results of these dynamics are larger amounts of cooler air sinking to the floors and, naturally, warmer air rising towards the ceilings. The better-insulated exterior walls of a SEE building limit the above exterior wall air movement dynamics. The result is much less difference between air temperatures near the floors and ceilings with a much more comfortable "feeling" to a room's temperature.

Just think, in SEE offices no more workers sitting at desks with electric heaters beside them in the winter or electric fans in the summer. Also, there will be much less complaining about having cool air in the summer or hot air in the winter constantly running and possibly blowing on them. In SEE homes, occupants can move around enjoying their homes without having to change the amount of clothing they wear for different rooms. Also there will be no need for dangerous portable electric heaters or noisy room air conditioners constantly running. SEE buildings are just plain more comfortable in which to work or live.

On a slight tangent, I would like to mention that radiant floor heating has recently seen an increasing demand here in Maine, especially for new homes. Homes with such a heating source also "feel" more comfortable. This is because such a system radiates heat up from the floor warming people's feet and legs. Many people are more familiar with living in NBC or non-SEE homes, which tend to generally make one's legs and feet feel cold in the winter because of the pooling of large amounts of cold air near the floor as mentioned above. The idea and feeling of having warmer legs and feet is what people find most appealing about radiant floor heating.

Potential new home clients often ask me about utilizing radiant slab heat in their new homes, when they are considering having me design and/or build a new home for them. I explain the different heating dynamics of a SEE home versus an NBC home (as mentioned above) and have generally convinced people to forgo such a heating system. The high cost of radiant floor heating also helps them decide not to go with such a heating system. I have yet to have a client for whom I have built a SEE home complain about the "feel" of their new home in cold weather. A radiant floor heating system would readily work in a SEE home; however, it is an extra expense that is not necessary for comfort reasons.

I also must mention that radiant floor heating systems are generally not very compatible with passive solar homes. Many of the homes (both SEE and non-SEE) that I have designed and built over the last thirty years have been passive solar. I have trouble not taking advantage of a free heating source such as the sun provides.

Radiant floor heating generally requires heating up the large thermal mass of a concrete slab and keeping it at a constant temperature. It usually takes at least a day for such a radiant heating system to "balance out" and evenly heat a home when it is first turned on. For this reason, it is also not recommended to try to have temperature setbacks for night times or during the day when the inhabitants may not be at home, as it could easily take up to an hour for the home's temperature to balance out again. Even setting the temperature back when one is going away for a weekend or vacation week may mean coming home to a cold house that could take up to a day to warm up.

A passive solar home can easily upset the balance of a radiant slab, as a large influx of solar heat gain on a sunny day will often overheat such a home. I do not see the opening of windows in the wintertime to cool such a passive solar home, as being an energy efficient activity. I also believe that massive thermal heaters such as "Russian" fireplaces (many other ethnic names are used for these heaters) can have somewhat similar compatibility problems with passive solar homes. However, many existing homes were not built with passive solar aspects and many new homes for various reasons cannot be built as passive solar homes, so radiant floor heat or thermal mass heat would be compatible with them.

The types of heating systems that I recommend for passive solar SEE homes are what I call "light" systems. By this, I mean heating systems that do not store large quantities of heat in thermo mass masonry or liquid containers open to the living area of a home. Such a system could be as simple as a natural gas or propane fired fireplace or Franklin-type stove. Such heaters come on when heat is needed and stay idle when the sun takes over. Electric heat would also be a good alternative if electric rates were competitive with gas or propane, which they currently are not in Maine.

SEE buildings are also much quieter than NBC or older existing structures. The blocking out of exterior sounds is the result of the extra insulation combined with double wall construction, which is similar to how a sound studio is built. The ICF's concrete/foam walls also have much better sound deadening qualities than NBC or older construction generally provides. In addition, SEE buildings also have much less internal mechanical heating/cooling noises, due to smaller systems that are generally quieter and less frequently called upon to operate than those of NBC or older existing structures.

43

Continuous and quiet low speed fans are utilized through an air-to-air heat exchanger to circulate clean air from the outside of SEE buildings, while removing stale air from the inside. This provides for a much healthier living or working environment with colds/flues less likely to be passed around between occupants. Such systems can also help to alleviate issues concerning mold or radon (a natural occurring radioactive gas that can escape from the ground).

Anyone who has ever lived in a SEE home that I have designed and/or built will confirm all that I have stated above. I am sure that people living in SEE homes built by others will also agree.

Chapter 10: WHO SHOULD SUPPORT SEE?

From what has been presented in the previous chapters, it should be obvious that WE ALL should support SEE. Even those parties one would think might oppose SEE, as discussed in the next chapter, really have good reasons to support SEE.

However, answering this chapter's title question in a bit more depth will provide a good review of SEE's many benefits and to specifically upon whom those benefits might be bestowed. Perhaps the deeper the understanding of SEE the more likely the benefactors will even establish a lobbing effort to promote SEE.

EVERYONE should support SEE for its economic, environmental, and geo/political benefits. It is also worth noting that, the economic benefits will not be relegated just to any "growth areas" of our country, but dispersed evenly throughout the country to wherever there are already existing homes and buildings.

Homeowners, apartment owners, and office building owners should support SEE for personal economic reasons. SEE homeowners will have more discretionary money to spend, invest or save. SEE building owners will have the potential for higher profits, better occupancy rates, and/or happier tenants or workers. Apartment renters should also support SEE to assure lower rental rates for the future.

Bankers should support SEE, because loan customers, building new or converting their existing older homes to SEE, should be more capable of paying their future mortgage or loan payments due to not having growing exorbitant energy costs. I personally know of a family who lost their home, because they chose to not freeze and paid for oil and food instead of their mortgage payment. The total cost of ownership for a SEE home is simply lower than for an NBC or older existing home and will continue and be even more so in the future. Bankers should also support other SEE building owners for similar reasons.

ALL construction workers, builders, and general contractors should support SEE, because it can provide them with much needed jobs almost immediately. Further, SEE conversions will start a whole new industry that will utilize their skills well into the future.

Construction materials suppliers (i.e.: lumber companies, Home Depot, Lowes, etc.) should support SEE as they will see a significant increase in the need for the materials that they supply and their sales should increase accordingly and again well into the future.

Construction materials manufacturers should support SEE, as they will have demand for the products that they produce increase immediately and continuously well into the future.

The transportation industry should support SEE, because they will be moving the large increase in materials that will be shipped to meet the demands for SEE well into the future.

Realtors should support SEE, because, if SEE is not adopted, there will be fewer people who can afford the total cost of ownership for a home. Home sales will continue to be down if not go into a long slow decline. The vibrant economy that SEE will produce in their markets, will mean more people being able to afford to buy homes - - SEE homes or homes that will be converted into SEE homes.

Environmentalists should support SEE for its ability to cutback on pollution. Exactly how adversely our polluting has affected our environment, what needs to be done to correct it, and how long it will take to do, are up for competing conjecture. Common sense alone should tell us, that we cannot indefinitely "dump our garbage out the back door" without it eventually affecting us negatively in some fashion.

46

Politicians should support SEE, because it is really the best thing for all of their constituents. Creating good jobs and improving the economy (locally or nationally) will help them get reelected. Improving the environment will also gain them support from another interest group in their constituency. Having a vibrant economy will also provide them with the income resources to improve other benefits for their constituents. Just think, promote SEE and all these things will happen without a great expense, if any, for their governments. Just taking the time to endorse the SEE effort may be all that is needed.

Governments should support SEE, because of the positive economic changes that SEE will immediately produce and will continue to produce for long into the future. I am sure that any government that simply promoted the positive effects that SEE promises, would be looked upon quite favorably by their constituents. Ideally, governments would take an even more active role in promoting the SEE transformation. Setting up simple rotating self-paying loan programs that could finance the SEE transformation would be one way, as well as possibly guaranteeing any loans that banks might make for SEE conversion projects. None of this would have to be in any way a form of a government "give away".

Governments might also want to adopt SEE for their own housing projects as well as for government buildings to keep the ever-increasing cost of energy for these projects in check.

The Federal Government especially could easily promote SEE through its already existing Energy Star Housing Program that already utilizes the HERS analysis process. That is why I choose the existing HERS network to evaluate SEE buildings. I just adopted the Energy Star Housing Program's highest level of performance (five stars), as I felt that I had proven with my own research and experience that such a standard would be relatively easy to achieve, was cost effective, and could pay for itself.

In summary, anyone should support SEE who will benefit from having more money to save or spend, anyone who will benefit from having a cleaner environment, anyone who will benefit from living where there is a vibrant economy, anyone who would like to live in a more geopolitically stable world, anyone who would like to live, work, and socialize in more physically comfortable homes and buildings, and finally anyone who would like to get elected or be re-elected to serve the public. I cannot understand how anyone would not want SEE for themselves and everyone else for all of the above reasons. Again, remember the "No brainer" comment of the high school students.

I am sure that I must have missed some beneficiaries of SEE, but I believe the point that I am trying to convey here has been well made.

Chapter 11: WHO MIGHT NOT SUPPORT SEE?

There may well be people who from their perspective may not view SEE as a good thing. People who work for companies that produce or supply energy might not support SEE, because they may fear SEE's adoption will cut into their sales and profits as well as maybe even take away their jobs. I do not view these fears as being very well founded.

My perspective is that SEE will not be implemented overnight, but over many years, if not a decade or two. My estimate is fifteen to at least twenty years. Energy sales will not plummet and there will certainly be plenty of time for energy companies to divert their resources into other profitable ventures. SEE, alone, will require a considerable amount of new insulation products - - especially for older existing buildings. It will take energy to manufacture this insulation, petroleum in particular to make foam products as well as new vinyl siding, and fuel consuming trucks to transport the materials. Even the traveling that construction workers alone will have to do traveling to and from jobs will increase demand for their fuel products.

The longer we can stretch out the use of our limited energy resources, the easier and less expensive it will be for us to make the changes to SEE and find suitable alternative forms of energy. Wait too long and we may not have the best materials and resources remaining to easily and economically convert to SEE.

We cannot continue to trash the Earth or humans may not have any viable and healthy places to live. The Earth's survival is assured no matter whatever we choose to do to it, but life, as we now know it, may not be. Again, remember that the destruction of the polar bears' environment is only the beginning. If the Earth's capability to support human life is reduced from eight billion to two billion, things will have to change dramatically and probably not pleasantly. Less people will also mean less demand for any types of energy - - clean, renewable, or otherwise.

Rising sea levels alone have the potential to significantly and adversely affect our society's infrastructure. Many of our coastal cities will be threatened along with their corresponding industries (factories, refineries, port facilities, resorts, nuclear plants, etc.). Unless sailing over the North Pole, fishing above Key West, or drilling for oil in the Antarctic are truly your goals, sea level rise, whether from the greenhouse effect or a natural Earth cycle, will not be good for any of us.

I would be very willing to discuss with anyone, any perceived negative aspects of SEE that they might have. Perhaps you can convince me of some, or perhaps I can convince you there aren't any.

Chapter 12: WHAT SHOULD YOU DO?

Well, I believe that I have thoroughly explained why "SEE (IS) The EMPOWERING Energy Solution". I expect people from all walks of life and levels of education to read this book. So that this book could be more easily read and understood, I have intentionally kept my explanation of and arguments for SEE as simple and as brief as possible.

I can certainly provide to anyone interested much more information in much more detail to support all that I have tried to briefly present. You and others can also independently confirm and/or prove all that I have presented.

I may be the first to express the ideas in this book and their interrelationships as completely and thoroughly as I have. Now, most of you who have read this book should have gained a good understanding of why I am so enthusiastic about SEE and all that it can do for us and our country and culture. You also should have a good idea of what could happen to our society, if we don't convert to utilizing the SEE concepts for all of our homes and buildings. That was my simple intent in writing this book - - to inform you of the SEE concept that I believe is good for ALL of us to begin adopting for our homes and buildings.

I personally have been living in evolving SEE homes and buildings since 1979. I have been advising my new home clients to have me design and build such homes for them since 1983, when I built my first SEE home. By the early 1990's, half of the homes that I was building were SEE homes. By the late 1990's, all of the homes that I was building were SEE homes. I doubt that I will ever be asked to design or construct any non-SEE homes or buildings in the future.

In the future, I will never live in a home that is not a SEE home, nor own a building that is not a SEE building. I should not have to explain my reasoning for this.

What should you do with the information that you now have? My simple advice is, "Do what is best for you - - financially, environmentally, locally, globally!" I know what your decisions will ultimately be. Some of you will just take advantage of what SEE has to offer sooner rather than later. Those who do it sooner will just be financially better off sooner and reap the comfort benefits of SEE sooner. The leadership of those early adopters will also go a long way towards promoting a brighter environmental and economic future of their communities and the world.

The late adopters will simply reap the personal benefits later.

If I could ask one thing from those of you who now have gained some understanding of SEE. **Please tell your family, friends, and co-workers about SEE, for their benefit as well as ours.** You may also feel compelled to tell others in positions to help promote the SEE concept - - bankers, realtors, and especially politicians or anyone in government. We all will benefit from SEE in the many ways presented in this book.

Others, businesses in particular, may perceive a benefit for their companies and industries in lobbying for SEE. I hope that I have given you some of the tools necessary and the logic with which to start this process. Don't hesitate to use me as a resource and contact me for more information about SEE. And, good luck with your efforts.

Thank you ALL for reading this and thank you in advance for building and converting your homes and buildings to SEE and supporting the SEE concept. I am sure my son and his contemporaries will also thank you for this in the future.

Chapter 13: OTHER SEE HOMES THAT I DESIGNED & BUILT

Following are pictures of some of the SEE homes that I have built over the years. I cannot stress how easy it is to adapt the double-wall concept to just about any type or style of home. The only visible difference is thicker walls that are evidenced by deeper windowsills and doorjambs.

Note that with the exception of the pre 1850's farmhouse, the homes all have a passive solar theme. There are two reasons for this. The first is that my initial construction company started out promoting passive solar as well as early SEE prototypes, so I am very familiar with how to incorporate passive solar into a SEE or any other type of home. The second reason is, as I have mentioned earlier, I find it difficult to not take advantage of the free energy that the Sun provides. I have found that almost every home site can take advantage of at least some passive solar energy.

Also note that several of the homes that I have designed as well as built have had octagonal themes (note three on the following pages). The last one pictured was my first. In designing and building that home I noticed how well the octagonal area worked from a passive solar aspect.

Later, I also realized the energy efficiency of the octagonal shape. A square is the most energy efficient rectangle with the least amount of exterior wall per square foot of interior living space. A ball would be the most energy efficient, albeit the hardest to construct. Buckminster Fuller's geodesic domes were a practical way of building a "ball" shaped structure. However, as hard as I have tried, I have never figured out an inexpensive and practical way to build one with a double-wall, which I feel would be necessary given the amount of thermal breaks in traditional geodesic dome construction.

An octagonal home I believe is a practical and cost effective compromise design between a square and a circular shaped building. A square building is 12.8% less efficient than a circular building with 12.8% more exterior wall per square foot of interior living space. An octagonal building, however, is only 2.8% less efficient than a circular building and considerably easier to build. Over the years I have designed dozens of single and multistory octagonal homes as well as one office building.

ICF Octagon NW Elevation
Harpswell , Maine

Double-wall SEE
Bristol, ME

Double-Wall SEE Octagon
Falmouth, Maine

Double-Wall SEE
Cumberland, Maine

Double-Wall SEE
Raymond, Maine

Double-Wall SEE
Falmouth, Maine

57

Double-Wall SEE (Frank Lloyd Wright Redo)
Brunswick, Maine

Housewright Double-Wall SEE
Windham, Maine

Gut Rehab SEE Retrofit pre 1850 farmhouse
Woodstock, Maine

Double-Wall / Double Rafter pre 1850 farmhouse
Woodstock, Maine

ICF Octagon S & SE Elevation
Harpswell , Maine

Double-Wall SEE Octagon Ranch with Wings
Gorham, Maine

AUTHOR'S BIOGRAPHY

Thomas A. Peterson grew up in Plymouth, Massachusetts. He received his BSBA in Business Management from Southeastern Massachusetts University (now University of Massachusetts – Dartmouth) in 1971. He continued his academic training receiving an MBA from Tulane University in New Orleans in 1973, where he specialized in Marketing.

He began his business career doing Marketing Research at the headquarters of major corporate retailers located in the Northeast - - including Hannaford Bros. Supermarkets in Maine, Wellby Drugstores in Maine, Grossman's & Moore's home centers in Massachusetts, Zayre discount department stores in Massachusetts, and T. J. Maxx clothing stores in Massachusetts. The majority of this work centered on doing field research and economic and population demographic research. He then wrote detailed reports and gave lengthy oral presentations to the top management of his various corporate employers.

His interest in utilizing solar energy began in 1975 when he started researching the basic concepts after the first "energy crisis" of the 1970's. In 1979, after the second 1970's energy crisis, he left the corporate retail world to design and build his own experimental solar home in the Portland, Maine area. That was soon followed by the formation of a construction company, Solar Design & Construction. SD&C, for short, began building Sunroom additions, Passive Solar homes, as well as conventional homes. In the beginning he built what is now considered to be heavily insulated buildings in Maine using 2x6 construction with six inches of fiberglass insulation. In the early 1980's he started to experiment with and utilize double-wall construction as well as other super insulation techniques and refined his passive solar designs. Thus, began the SEE odyssey. Realizing that most people have limited funds, his designs have always emphasized cost containment.

Paralleling his construction career, he began teaching Marketing and Management courses, first at St. Joseph's College in Windham, Maine then at the University of Southern Maine In the Portland/Gorham area. Teaching as both a full-time and part-time professor, he honed his presentation skills. He later helped develop government sponsored export seminar programs for both Canadian Federal and Provincial Governments for experienced businesses in the Canadian Maritime Provinces of New Brunswick & Nova Scotia.

As his knowledge of passive solar and super insulation grew, he also began to market these concepts through his company with written articles and company pamphlets, and by conducting seminars of these concepts at home shows.

In his more recent attempt to market two SEE homes built on speculation in Windham, Maine, he researched all the current information and programs that were available to promote such dwellings. He was amazed at what government and private support information and programs were available, such as the Energy Star Housing and LEEDS programs.

He was also amazed at the almost total lack of awareness of the information with the general public, realtors, local governments, and various housing related institutions (banks, mortgage companies, etc.). In doing further financial research, he was also amazed that SEE homes could more than cover the extra financing costs to build them. A SEE home the first year built, when financed with a conventional mortgage, would have annual energy cost savings greater than the extra financing costs to cover meeting SEE standards. He also explored and developed ways to convert older existing homes and buildings to SEE standards.

He then looked at all of the information that he had gathered and saw that a very compelling argument could easily be made for building every home in the United States as a SEE home and further renovating every existing home to SEE standards. He also found that none of this information was put together anywhere in a complete and comprehensive package that could sell the concept as a major solution to greenhouse gas pollution as well as a way to save on energy use and rising energy costs for the future economic stability of the United States.

He believes that given our current slump in construction, the retrofitting of existing housing could provide tens if not hundreds of thousands of construction jobs immediately - - with a lot more to follow.

Given the deteriorating condition of our environment, the economy, and the continually rising costs of energy, he feels that it is important to pass on all that he has learned about SEE housing to others in as timely a fashion as possible. His solutions to those problems are the reason for the writing of this book.

APPENDICES

Notes:

Appendix A

ENERGY SAVINGS - New SEE Home VS. New NBC Home
Years 1-30:

1/18/12

Year	Annual Energy Expenses (1) New SEE	New NBC	Annual Savings For SEE Home	Annual Mortgage P. & I. @ 5% $220K SEE Home	Add $20K - SEE	SEE's Net Annual Savings (Sav - Add Int)	CUMULATIVE SAVINGS For a SEE Home
1	$1,000.00	$4,000.00	$3,000.00	$14,172.12	$1,288.32	$1,711.68	$1,711.68
2	$1,120.00	$4,480.00	$3,360.00	$14,172.12	$1,288.32	$2,071.68	$3,783.36
3	$1,254.40	$5,017.60	$3,763.20	$14,172.12	$1,288.32	$2,474.88	$6,258.24
4	$1,404.93	$5,619.71	$4,214.78	$14,172.12	$1,288.32	$2,926.46	$9,184.70
5	$1,573.52	$6,294.08	$4,720.56	$14,172.12	$1,288.32	$3,432.24	$12,616.94
6	$1,762.34	$7,049.37	$5,287.03	$14,172.12	$1,288.32	$3,998.71	$16,615.65
7	$1,973.82	$7,895.29	$5,921.47	$14,172.12	$1,288.32	$4,633.15	$21,248.80
8	$2,210.68	$8,842.73	$6,632.04	$14,172.12	$1,288.32	$5,343.72	$26,592.52
9	$2,475.96	$9,903.85	$7,427.89	$14,172.12	$1,288.32	$6,139.57	$32,732.09
10	$2,773.08	$11,092.32	$8,319.24	$14,172.12	$1,288.32	$7,030.92	$39,763.01
11	$3,105.85	$12,423.39	$9,317.54	$14,172.12	$1,288.32	$8,029.22	$47,792.23
12	$3,478.55	$13,914.20	$10,435.65	$14,172.12	$1,288.32	$9,147.33	$56,939.56
13	$3,895.98	$15,583.90	$11,687.93	$14,172.12	$1,288.32	$10,399.61	$67,339.17
14	$4,363.49	$17,453.97	$13,090.48	$14,172.12	$1,288.32	$11,802.16	$79,141.33
15	$4,887.11	$19,548.45	$14,661.34	$14,172.12	$1,288.32	$13,373.02	$92,514.34
16	$5,473.57	$21,894.26	$16,420.70	$14,172.12	$1,288.32	$15,132.38	$107,646.72
17	$6,130.39	$24,521.57	$18,391.18	$14,172.12	$1,288.32	$17,102.86	$124,749.58
18	$6,866.04	$27,464.16	$20,598.12	$14,172.12	$1,288.32	$19,309.80	$144,059.38
19	$7,689.97	$30,759.86	$23,069.90	$14,172.12	$1,288.32	$21,781.58	$165,840.96
20	$8,612.76	$34,451.05	$25,838.29	$14,172.12	$1,288.32	$24,549.97	$190,390.93
21	$9,646.29	$38,585.17	$28,938.88	$14,172.12	$1,288.32	$27,650.56	$218,041.49
22	$10,803.85	$43,215.39	$32,411.54	$14,172.12	$1,288.32	$31,123.22	$249,164.71
23	$12,100.31	$48,401.24	$36,300.93	$14,172.12	$1,288.32	$35,012.61	$284,177.32
24	$13,552.35	$54,209.39	$40,657.04	$14,172.12	$1,288.32	$39,368.72	$323,546.04
25	$15,178.63	$60,714.52	$45,535.89	$14,172.12	$1,288.32	$44,247.57	$367,793.61
26	$17,000.06	$68,000.26	$51,000.19	$14,172.12	$1,288.32	$49,711.87	$417,505.48
27	$19,040.07	$76,160.29	$57,120.22	$14,172.12	$1,288.32	$55,831.90	$473,337.38
28	$21,324.88	$85,299.52	$63,974.64	$14,172.12	$1,288.32	$62,686.32	$536,023.70
29	$23,883.87	$95,535.47	$71,651.60	$14,172.12	$1,288.32	$70,363.28	$606,386.98
30	$26,749.93	$106,999.72	$80,249.79	$14,172.12	$1,288.32	$78,961.47	$685,348.45
Total	$241,332.68	$965,330.74	$723,998.05	$425,163.60	$38,649.60	$685,348.45	

(1) Assumes energy costs will increase at an annual rate of 12%

67

Notes:

Appendix B

ENERGY SAVINGS FOR A NEW HOME BUILT TO SEE STANDARDS
& RETURN ON INVESTMENT (ROI) ANALYSIS:

1/25/12

Year	Annual Energy Expenses (1) New SEE (2)	New NBC	Annual Savings For SEE Home Over NBC Home	ROI on Added Cost of SEE ($20,000.00)
1	$1,000.00	$4,000.00	$3,000.00	15.00%
2	$1,120.00	$4,480.00	$3,360.00	16.80%
3	$1,254.40	$5,017.60	$3,763.20	18.82%
4	$1,404.93	$5,619.71	$4,214.78	21.07%
5	$1,573.52	$6,294.08	$4,720.56	23.60%
6	$1,762.34	$7,049.37	$5,287.03	26.44%
7	$1,973.82	$7,895.29	$5,921.47	29.61%
8	$2,210.68	$8,842.73	$6,632.04	33.16%
9	$2,475.96	$9,903.85	$7,427.89	37.14%
10	$2,773.08	$11,092.32	$8,319.24	41.60%
Cum. 1-10	$17,548.74	$70,194.94	$52,646.21	
11	$3,105.85	$12,423.39	$9,317.54	46.59%
12	$3,478.55	$13,914.20	$10,435.65	52.18%
13	$3,895.98	$15,583.90	$11,687.93	58.44%
14	$4,363.49	$17,453.97	$13,090.48	65.45%
15	$4,887.11	$19,548.45	$14,661.34	73.31%
16	$5,473.57	$21,894.26	$16,420.70	82.10%
17	$6,130.39	$24,521.57	$18,391.18	91.96%
18	$6,866.04	$27,464.16	$20,598.12	102.99%
19	$7,689.97	$30,759.86	$23,069.90	115.35%
20	$8,612.76	$34,451.05	$25,838.29	129.19%
Cum. 1-20	$72,052.44	$288,209.77	$216,157.33	
21	$9,646.29	$38,585.17	$28,938.88	144.69%
22	$10,803.85	$43,215.39	$32,411.54	162.06%
23	$12,100.31	$48,401.24	$36,300.93	181.50%
24	$13,552.35	$54,209.39	$40,657.04	203.29%
25	$15,178.63	$60,714.52	$45,535.89	227.68%
26	$17,000.06	$68,000.26	$51,000.19	255.00%
27	$19,040.07	$76,160.29	$57,120.22	285.60%
28	$21,324.88	$85,299.52	$63,974.64	319.87%
29	$23,883.87	$95,535.47	$71,651.60	358.26%
30	$26,749.93	$106,999.72	$80,249.79	401.25%
Cum. 1-30	$258,881.42	$1,035,525.68	$776,644.26	

(1) Assumes energy costs will increase at an annual rate of 12%
(2) Assumes an 75%% reduction in energy use over an NBC home.

Notes:

Appendix C

BREAKEVEN ANALYSIS
FOR AN OLDER EXISTING HOME
CONVERTED TO SEE VS. UNCONVERTED: 1/27/12

Year	Annual Energy Expenses (1) Converted to SEE (2)	Unconverted	Annual Savings For SEE Home	Savings Available For Flinancing Costs	BREAKEVEN $$$$ To Finance That Savings Would Cover 15 Year @ 5%	30 Year @ 5%
1	$1,000.00	$6,000.00	$5,000.00	$5,000.00	$52,700.00	$77,600.00
2	$1,120.00	$6,720.00	$5,600.00	$5,600.00	$59,000.00	$87,000.00
3	$1,254.40	$7,526.40	$6,272.00	$6,272.00	$66,100.00	$97,300.00
4	$1,404.93	$8,429.57	$7,024.64	$7,024.64	$74,000.00	$109,100.00
5	$1,573.52	$9,441.12	$7,867.60	$7,867.60	$83,000.00	$122,100.00
6	$1,762.34	$10,574.05	$8,811.71	$8,811.71	$93,000.00	$136,800.00
7	$1,973.82	$11,842.94	$9,869.11	$9,869.11	$104,000.00	$153,200.00
8	$2,210.68	$13,264.09	$11,053.41	$11,053.41	$116,500.00	$171,600.00
9	$2,475.96	$14,855.78	$12,379.82	$12,379.82	$130,500.00	$192,200.00
10	$2,773.08	$16,638.47	$13,865.39	$13,865.39	$146,100.00	$215,200.00
Cumulative 1-10	$17,548.74	$105,292.41	$87,743.68			
11	$3,105.85	$18,635.09	$15,529.24	$15,529.24	$163,700.00	$241,200.00
12	$3,478.55	$20,871.30	$17,392.75	$17,392.75	$183,300.00	$270,000.00
13	$3,895.98	$23,375.86	$19,479.88	$19,479.88	$205,100.00	$302,400.00
14	$4,363.49	$26,180.96	$21,817.47	$21,817.47	$230,000.00	$338,700.00
15	$4,887.11	$29,322.67	$24,435.56	$24,435.56	$257,500.00	$379,300.00
16	$5,473.57	$32,841.39	$27,367.83	$27,367.83	$288,400.00	$424,900.00
17	$6,130.39	$36,782.36	$30,651.97	$30,651.97	$323,000.00	$475,800.00
18	$6,866.04	$41,196.25	$34,330.20	$34,330.20	$361,700.00	$533,000.00
19	$7,689.97	$46,139.79	$38,449.83	$38,449.83	$405,200.00	$597,000.00
20	$8,612.76	$51,676.57	$43,063.81	$43,063.81	$453,800.00	$668,500.00
Cumulative 1-20	$72,052.44	$432,314.65	$360,262.21			
25	$15,178.63	$91,071.77	$75,893.14	$75,893.14	$799,800.00	$379,300.00
30	$26,749.93	$160,499.58	$133,749.65	$133,749.65	$1,409,500.00	$2,076,000.00
Cumulative 1-30	$241,332.68	$1,447,996.11	$1,206,663.42			

(1)   Assumes energy costs will increase at an annual rate of 12%
(2)   Assumes an 83.33% reduction in energy use.

Notes:

Appendix D

ENERGY SAVINGS FOR AN EXISTING HOME CONVERTED TO SEE VS.
UNCONVERTED & RETURN ON INVESTMENT (ROI) ANALYSIS:

1/28/12

Year	Annual Energy Costs (1) Converted to SEE (2)	Unconverted	Annual Savings For SEE Home	Cost of SEE Conversion (Investment) $50,000.00 ROI	$75,000.00 ROI
1	$1,000.00	$6,000.00	$5,000.00	10.00%	6.67%
2	$1,120.00	$6,720.00	$5,600.00	11.20%	7.47%
3	$1,254.40	$7,526.40	$6,272.00	12.54%	8.36%
4	$1,404.93	$8,429.57	$7,024.64	14.05%	9.37%
5	$1,573.52	$9,441.12	$7,867.60	15.74%	10.49%
6	$1,762.34	$10,574.05	$8,811.71	17.62%	11.75%
7	$1,973.82	$11,842.94	$9,869.11	19.74%	13.16%
8	$2,210.68	$13,264.09	$11,053.41	22.11%	14.74%
9	$2,475.96	$14,855.78	$12,379.82	24.76%	16.51%
10	$2,773.08	$16,638.47	$13,865.39	27.73%	18.49%
11	$3,105.85	$18,635.09	$15,529.24	31.06%	20.71%
12	$3,478.55	$20,871.30	$17,392.75	34.79%	23.19%
13	$3,895.98	$23,375.86	$19,479.88	38.96%	25.97%
14	$4,363.49	$26,180.96	$21,817.47	43.63%	29.09%
15	$4,887.11	$29,322.67	$24,435.56	48.87%	32.58%
16	$5,473.57	$32,841.39	$27,367.83	54.74%	36.49%
17	$6,130.39	$36,782.36	$30,651.97	61.30%	40.87%
18	$6,866.04	$41,196.25	$34,330.20	68.66%	45.77%
19	$7,689.97	$46,139.79	$38,449.83	76.90%	51.27%
20	$8,612.76	$51,676.57	$43,063.81	86.13%	57.42%
21	$9,646.29	$57,877.76	$48,231.47	96.46%	64.31%
22	$10,803.85	$64,823.09	$54,019.24	108.04%	72.03%
23	$12,100.31	$72,601.86	$60,501.55	121.00%	80.67%
24	$13,552.35	$81,314.08	$67,761.74	135.52%	90.35%
25	$15,178.63	$91,071.77	$75,893.14	151.79%	101.19%
26	$17,000.06	$102,000.39	$85,000.32	170.00%	113.33%
27	$19,040.07	$114,240.43	$95,200.36	190.40%	126.93%
28	$21,324.88	$127,949.28	$106,624.40	213.25%	142.17%
29	$23,883.87	$143,303.20	$119,419.33	238.84%	159.23%
30	$26,749.93	$160,499.58	$133,749.65	267.50%	178.33%
Cumulative 1-30	$241,332.68	$1,447,996.11	$1,206,663.42		

(1)   Assumes energy costs will increase at an annual rate of 12%
(2)   Assumes an 83.33% reduction in energy use.

73

www.ingramcontent.com/pod-product-compliance
Lightning Source LLC
Chambersburg PA
CBHW071623170526
45166CB00003B/1172